Types and Shadows
And Interesting Old Testament Parallels

By
Matt Hennecke

ISBN 10: 1-58427-397-6
ISBN 13: 978-1-58427-397-4

Guardian of Truth Foundation
CEI Bookstore
220 S. Marion St., Athens, AL 35611
1-855-492-6657
www.CEIbooks.com

truth
BOOKS

www.CEIbooks.com

If you have questions about this
workbook please contact Matt Hennecke at
matt@biblemaps.com

CONTENTS

LESSON 1: What Are Types and Shadows?   5

LESSON 2: In the Garden: A Plan for Sin   9

LESSON 3: The Ark: God and Water   13

LESSON 4: Undoing of Babel: The Power of the Word   17

LESSON 5: Christ Foreshadowed in Joseph and Moses   21

LESSON 6: The Amalekites: The Threat of Satan and Sin   25

LESSON 7: Christ the Rock in the Old Testament   29

LESSON 8: The Tabernacle as a Type   33

LESSON 9: Worship Types: The Ark of the Covenant   37

LESSON 10: Leprosy: The Horror of Sin   41

LESSON 11: Rahab in Rehab: Salvation in Jericho   45

LESSON 12: Cities of Refuge: Finding Solace in Christ   49

LESSON 13: Mephibosheth: The Grace of a King   53

Answer Key   57

*Therefore the Law has become our tutor to lead us
to Christ, so that we may be justified by faith.*
- Galatians 3:24

*...the Law, since it is only a shadow of the good things
to come and not the very form of things, can never, by
the same sacrifices which they offer continually year by
year, make perfect those who draw near.*
- Hebrews 10:1

WHAT ARE TYPES AND SHADOWS?

As a grandfather I have had many opportunities to read to my grandchildren. They love books. It's not unusual for Peter or Carter (Graham is still a bit too small) to grab a favorite book, climb up into my lap, and snuggle in for a bedtime story. They have many books but some are their favorites and they repeatedly ask me to read those books.

Sometimes as I read aloud I realize the author of the book has hidden a moral or lesson in its pages. In other words, while there is a "surface" story involving a cat, or a truck, or a farm family, beneath it is a more important story – a lesson of life – that conveys a deeper truth about honesty, the importance of sharing, or even about true friendship.

Often as I continue reading I wonder if Peter and Carter are grasping the deeper lessons. Do they "see" the deeper message, or are they (because they're still children) entranced by the surface story and miss the deeper message? Then I wonder this: is it possible that the deeper message is somehow finding its way into their developing minds without them even consciously being aware of it?

The scenario I describe above is exactly what I mean when I talk about Old Testament "types" and "shadows." Those of us who were brought up hearing "stories" from the Bible about Adam, Noah, Joseph, Moses, and Ruth were hearing stories of real men and women, but just beneath the surface of those "stories" were often lessons to be learned about Jesus Christ. One writer put it this way: The Old Testament is a sort of kindergarten in which God's people are trained in divine things, by which they are led to look for better things to come in Christ. Paul was making this very point when he said, *"...the law was our schoolmaster to bring us unto Christ"* (Gal. 3:24).

Types and shadows, then, are Old Testament people, events, items, or ceremonies that *foreshadow* the coming Messiah and His church. In many ways, the Old Testament was *"...a mere shadow of what is to come; but the substance belongs to Christ"* (Col. 2:17).

> A type is some outward or sensible thing ordained of God under the Old Testament to represent and hold forth something of Christ in the New.
>
> - Samuel Mather

In this study we will embark on a journey of discovery to see what we might learn of Jesus the Christ, His church, and God's plan of redemption hidden in the pages of the Old Testament. I hope you find it enlightening.

- Matt Hennecke, September 27, 2015

For Study and Discussion

1. Why do you think God used types and shadows in the Old Testament to reveal what was coming in the New Testament?

2. List below what you believe to be the two most obvious Old Testament types or shadows.

1

2

3. What are the characteristics of literal shadows that may help us better understand how to interpret biblical shadows?

"God in the types of the last dispensation was teaching His children their letters. In this dispensation He is teaching them to put the letters together, and they find that the letters, arrange them as they will, spell Christ, and nothing but Christ."   -Unknown

Some Terminology

The Old Testament person, event, item, or ceremony that foreshadows something in the New Testament is called the "type" while the person or thing of greater substance in the New Testament is called the "antitype." We tend to think of the prefix "anti" as meaning *something against* or *opposed to*, and indeed that is one meaning, but the meaning conveyed by the prefix in the word "antitype" is something *corresponding to*, or the *flip-side*. The idea conveyed by "antitype," then, is more like a person's reflection in a mirror.

TYPE ◀━━━ **The OT Shadow**

ANTITYPE ◀━━━ **The NT Reality**

4. Complete the chart below by indicating what the Old Testament story, event, or person foreshadowed in the New Testament.

OT "Type" that Foreshadows	NT Reality the "Antitype"	Reference
Jacob's ladder Gen. 28:11-19		John 1:51
Melchizedek Gen. 14:18-20		Heb. 7:1-22
Circumcision Gen. 17:9-11		Col. 2:11-12
Egyptian bondage Exod. 1:13-14		Rom. 6:22
Manna Exod. 16:1-4		John 6:48-50
The brazen serpent Num. 21:7-9		John 3:14-16
Jonah in the fish Jonah 1:16-17		Matt. 12:39-40

In the Old Testament the New lies hid.
In the New Testament, the meaning
of the Old becomes clear.
- Augustine

A QUEST TO FIND JESUS
The Way We Should Study the Bible

There is much talk these days about how one should go about reading and interpreting Scripture. The term used to describe the methodologies one might use to understand and interpret biblical texts is called "hermeneutics." Many of us have grown up applying at least one hermeneutic as it relates to establishing authority. We look at the New Testament to learn what is authorized by God by considering commands, approved examples, and necessary inferences.

Paul, as he writes to the Galatians suggests another hermeneutic we should use when reading the Old Testament when he says, *"the Law has become our tutor to lead us to Christ, so that we may be justified by faith"* (Gal. 3:24). In other words, our study of the Old Testament should be a study to find Jesus Christ in its pages.

Frank Viola in "Beyond Bible Study: Finding Jesus in Scripture" referred to this methodology as the "Christological hermeneutic." He went on to say that the goal of this approach to Bible study is to "find Jesus Christ in all of Scripture," and that "all of Scripture has but one center of gravity that links all of it together, and that center of gravity is the Person of Jesus Christ."

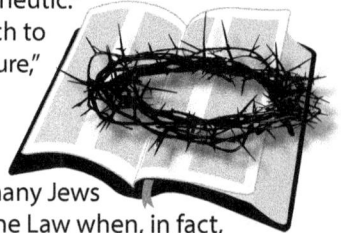

It is compelling to note that Jesus chided many Jews in His day because they sought eternal life in the Law when, in fact, the primary purpose of the Law was to testify of Him: *"You search the Scriptures because you think that in them you have eternal life; it is these that testify about Me"* (John 5:39).

Imagine how a study of the Old Testament would come alive if we would constantly be watching for Christ in its notable men and women of faith, its ceremonies, its feasts, even in the tabernacle and its furniture. There can be no doubt: the Bible is one story and that story is Christ!

For Discussion
Is it possible to read too much into an event and see a types or a shadow where none exists or was intended?

GOD'S PLAN FOR DEALING WITH SIN

GRACE IN THE GARDEN

The Bible doesn't tell us how long Adam and Eve enjoyed the wonders of the Garden of Eden before they succumbed to sin. It may have been weeks, months, or even years. Sadly, I'm inclined to think it wasn't very long at all. If history is any indication, humankind gives in to sin fairly quickly and perhaps it was mere days after the Lord's fruit-eating prohibition that Adam and Eve sinned. However long it was, Satan no doubt began his temptations soon after the completion of the "very good" (Gen. 1:31) creation, and didn't let up until he had seemingly ruined everything.

The story of the bliss and beauty of the garden is one that most have heard from an early age and it has been the subject of countless books and movies. One of the most notable works of literature, *Paradise Lost*, by John Milton captures the essense of the Fall and even alludes to God's redemptive plan in the opening five lines of the epic poem:

> *Of man's first disobedience, and the fruit*
> *of that forbidden tree, whose mortal taste*
> *Brought death into the world, and all our woe,*
> *with loss of Eden, till one greater Man*
> *Restore us, and regain the blissful seat....*

The question has often been asked, "Did God know *before* the first sin that a plan would be needed to redeem mankind?" There are several passages in Scripture that suggest He did. Consider Isaiah 46:9-10: "*I am God, and there is no other; I am God, and there is none like me, **declaring the end from the beginning** and from ancient time things not yet done, saying, 'My counsel shall stand, and I will accomplish all my purpose....'*"

Ephesians 1:4, 5 also suggests He did when it says: "*He chose us in Him **before** the foundation of the world....He **predestined** us to adoption as sons.*" Perhaps one need look no further than the garden "story" itself to see God was already at work to reveal His plan in the way He dealt with Adam and Eve's transgression in eating the forbidden fruit.

For Study and Discussion

1. Even while we were in our sin, who came seeking us (Luke 19:10)? Did he know the desperate state we were in (Rom. 5:8)? Who is included in his mission? Who is excluded?

Who is like the Lord our God, the One who sits enthroned on high,

Who stoops down to look on the heavens and the earth?

He raises the poor from the dust and lifts the needy from the ash heap;

He seats them with princes, with the princes of his people.

- Psalm 113:5-8

2. Christ came revealing what three amazing attributes of God? (See Eph. 2:4-5.)

He is a God of...

He is a God of...

He is a God of...

3. In your own words define each of the three attributes below.

4. How does the Lord *draw* us to Himself and salvation (2 Thess. 2:14; 2 Tim. 1:8-9)?

Cecil F. Alexander, 1852 and William H. Jude, 1887

Jesus Calls Us; O'er the Tumult

5. According to John 16:8 what did Jesus say was the purpose of the Holy Spirit? In what way is His purpose similar to that of the Law? (See Gal. 3:19.)

6. In what way does God express His love toward us that may seem to some people at odds with love? (See Heb. 12:5-6; Job 5:17.)

7. What two words does Paul use in describing those who are "blessed"? (See Rom. 4:7.)

They are...	They are...

8. According to Galatians 3:27 what has one figuratively done when baptized into Christ?

I will rejoice greatly in the LORD,
My soul will exult in my God;
For He has clothed me with garments
of salvation,
He has wrapped me with a robe of
righteousness.
- Isaiah 61:10

NOTE: We will complete the chart below during class:

The Shadow	The Substance
Genesis 3:8	Luke 19:10; Eph.2:4-5 He _____ to us.
Genesis 3:9	2 Thess. 2:13-14; 2 Tim. 1:8-9 He _____ to us.
Genesis 3:11	Gal. 3:19; John 16:8 He _____ us.
Genesis 3:14-19	Heb. 12:5-6 He _____ us.
Genesis 3:21	Rom. 4:7; Gal. 3:27 He _____ us.

What is prophetically significant about this?

The Book of God, the God of Books

The more you read the Bible and the more you meditate upon it, the more you will be astonished with it. He who is but a casual reader of the Bible does not know the height, the depth, the length, and breadth of the mighty meanings contained in its pages.

There are certain times when I discover a new vein of thought and I put my hand to my head and say in astonishment, "Oh, it is wonderful – I never saw this before in the Scriptures." You will find the Scriptures enlarge as you enter them; the more you study them the less you will appear to know of them for they widen out as we approach them. Especially will you find this the case with the "typical" parts of God's Word. Most of the historical books were intended to be types either of dispensations or experiences or offices of Jesus Christ. Study the Bible with this as a key and you will not blame the theologian, George Herbert, when he calls it "not only the book of God, but the God of books."

– from *Christ our Passover,* a sermon delivered by Charles Spurgeon, December 2, 1855.

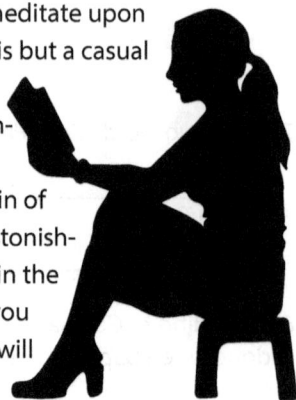

For Discussion: Are the similarities of the garden events to Christ's work in saving sinners merely coincidental or truly a type of His redemptive work?

Would telling the "story" of God's grace as revealed in the garden be an effective approach to teach someone about God's plan of salvation? How might recounting the garden-grace "story" help get past someone's defenses? What story did Nathan tell as a means of getting past David's defenses (2 Sam. 12:1-15)?

GOD AND WATER

THE ARK & SALVATION

According to D.H. Collins and H.M. Morris of the Creation Research Society, the exact dimensions of the ark provided superior design. Even in 210 knot winds – three times hurricane force – Noah's ark would have been very stable.

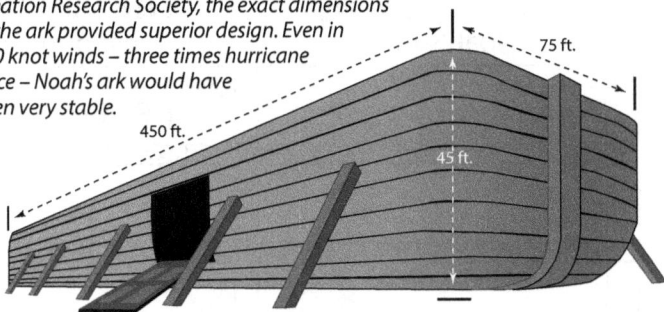

75 ft.

450 ft.

45 ft.

The story of Noah and his family's salvation in the ark is arguably the best known Bible "story" of all time. The events are known by those who never attend religious worship ser- vices and never open a Bible. Even Hollywood movie makers are somewhat familiar with the cataclysmic flood story.

The ancient events involving Noah and his family are the subject of controversy: Did the events really happen or is it a myth? Could the world be completely covered by water? Would the ark accommodate all the animals Noah took aboard? How did Noah's family keep the ark clean? If the questions aren't enough, there are the frequent supposed "ark sightings" high in the mountains of Turkey near Mt. Ararat.

For serious Bible students such questions and controversy miss the point of the story entirely. Moses didn't write of the flood to provide an engaging story to tell our children at bed-time or to create controversy. So why are the events recorded? Is there a deeper more important message con-tained in its telling that reveals truths about the human con-dition and the hope of salvation that awaits the faithful? If so, what are those lessons?

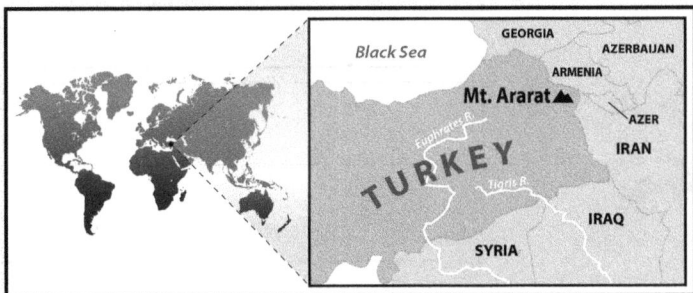

Black Sea

GEORGIA

AZERBAIJAN

ARMENIA

Mt. Ararat ▲

AZER

TURKEY

Euphrates R.

Tigris R.

IRAN

IRAQ

SYRIA

For Study and Discussion

1. Read the story of Noah and the ark (Gen. 6:5-7:24) then complete the chart below indicating as many similarities as you can between the events involving the ark and the characteristics of Christ or the church. One similarity is provided to get you started.

THE SHADOW Noah's Ark	THE SUBSTANCE Christ or the Church
Gen. 6:13-14 1 Builder - Noah	Matt.16:13-20 1 Builder - Christ

2. Noah and his family were saved through what element according to 1 Peter 3:20? What effect did that element have on those *outside* the ark?

3. List below other biblical events, stories, or verses that reveal both the *saving* and *destroying* power of water.

4. Noah was told to cover the ark inside and outside with pitch. Do some research about the Hebrew word translated "pitch." How is the same Hebrew word used elsewhere in the Old Testament? Is there any significance to the use of pitch in the salvation of Noah's family? How might it relate to our salvation?

5. What was pitch designed to do or accomplish? How might this relate to the work of Christ or of the Lord's church?

Cyprian, a third century bishop, citing the passage in 1 Peter 3:18-22, said, *"In saying this, Peter proves with his testimony that the one ark of Noah was a type of the one church."* Later he said, *"there is no salvation outside the church...."* The implication of this interpretation of the church is that only those "in" the church are or will be saved. One becomes a member of the church universal – the body of Christ – through baptism.

A Word About Gopher Wood

The ark was made of "gopher" wood (Gen. 6:14). Because this verse is the only place in the Old Testament where that Hebrew word appears, its meaning is obscure. Some think it was related to cypress or pine, others that "gopher" is a corruption of the Hebrew word "kopher" which is translated "pitch," thus referring either to wood with much sap in it, or wood later "pitched" for water-proofing.

Lessons from Noah and the Ark

Years ago a man by the name of Robert Fulghum wrote a book of short essays called *All I Really Need to Know I Learned in Kindergarten*. It was so popular it stirred a number people to imitate Fulghum's efforts with lists of their own. One such spinoff was entitled "All I Need to Know I Learned from Noah's Ark." Amongst its offerings were the following bits of sage advice:

1. Don't miss the boat.
2. Remember we are all in the same boat.
3. Plan ahead. It wasn't raining when Noah built the Ark.
4. Stay fit. When you're old someone may ask you to do something really big.
5. Don't listen to critics, just get on with the job that needs to be done.
6. Build your future on high ground.
7. For safety's sake travel in pairs.
8. Speed isn't everything. The snails were on board with the cheetahs.
9. When you're stressed, float awhile.
10. Remember the Ark was built by amateurs, the Titanic by professionals.

While these ten "lessons" are funny they miss the more important lesson of life revealed in the events of Noah's salvation. Just as Noah and his family had to be "in" the ark to be saved, we must be "in" Christ to be saved. How then do we get in Christ? Paul tells us in Romans 6:3 – *"Do you not know that all of us who have been baptized into Christ Jesus were baptized into his death?"* Again in Galatians 3:27 he says, *"For all of you who were baptized into Christ have clothed yourselves with Christ."*

For Discussion: Are the similarities between the story of the ark and the story of Christ and the church merely coincidental or intentional?

If the ark is a "type" then what is the "antitype" – Christ or the church, or both?

THE POWER OF THE WORD

UNDOING BABEL

Have you ever heard of Esperanto? It's a language that was developed between1877 and 1885 by Dr. Ludwig Lazarus Zamenhof, an ophthalmologist living in Warsaw, Poland. Dr. Zamenhof's goal was to create an easy-to-learn, politically neutral language that would transcend nationality and foster peace and international understanding between people with different languages. He was convinced a common language would resolve many of the problems that lead to strife and conflict in the world. It was his hope Esperanto would become the universal language uniting all the people throughout the world. The name "Esperanto" means "one who hopes," and currently it is estimated some 2 million people from many countries speak Esperanto.

To give you an idea of the "look" of the language, consider the passage below:

Rigard, ili estas unu popolo, kaj ili ĉiuj havas la saman lingvon. Kaj tio ili komencis far, kaj hodiaŭ nenio kiu ili celo fari estos neebla por ili.

Tial la Lordo disigita ilin eksterlande de tie super la vizaĝo de la tuta tero; kaj ili haltis konstruaĵon la urbon. Sekve sia(n) nomo nomiĝis Babelon, ĉar tie la Lordo konfuzis la lingvon de la tuta tero; kaj de tie la Lordo disigita ilin eksterlande super la vizaĝo de la tuta tero.

Any of the above words look familiar to you? Would you be frustrated if you had to try to decipher the language?

The origin of the many world languages can be traced, of course, to the "story" of Babel recorded in Genesis 11.

Why is the story of God confounding the people provided for us? Are there lessons we are to learn beyond the lessons of disobedience and pride? Do the events somehow correlate to some future event in God's plan of redemption for mankind?

Artist: Pieter Bruegel the Elder (1525 – 1569)

For Study and Discussion

1. According to Hebrews 4:12; Acts 11:14; and John 1:1,14, what is one of the most powerful forces in the world?

2. What unified the people in the events revealed in Genesis 11? Is that which unified them really that powerful in shaping behavior? Explain. (See Neh. 13:24.)

3. What materials did the people use in their construction project (v. 3)?

4. What was "raised up" by the people (v. 4)?

5. What were they intent on building and what did they want for themselves (v. 4)? To where did they want their tower to reach (v. 4)? What was their motivation?

6. What did God do specifically to stop the efforts of the people (v. 7)?

It is believed Babel was a ziggurat which were a form of temple common to the Sumerians, Babylonians, and Assyrians of ancient Mesopotamia.

Build in receding tiers upon a rectangular, oval, or square platform, the ziggurat was a pyramidal structure. Sun-baked bricks made up the core of the structure with facings of fired bricks on the outside. The facings were often glazed in different colors and may have had astrological significance.

The number of tiers typically ranged from two to seven, with a shrine or temple at the summit. Access to the shrine was provided by a series of ramps on one side of the ziggurat or by a spiral ramp from base to summit.

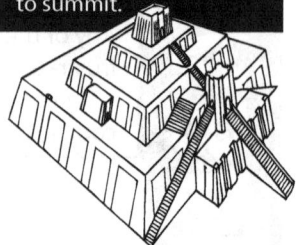

The Hebrew word for "tower" in Genesis 11: 4 is "migdal." The same word is used in Micah 4:8. To what does the word refer in Micah's prophecy?

7. What happened as a result of God's intervention (v. 8)?

8. Are we to learn more from the story of Babel than God's reaction to disobedience and pride? If so, what else are we to learn?

Complete the chart:

	SHADOW Babel (Genesis 11:1-9)		SUBSTANCE Pentecost (Acts 2:1-12)	
What unified the people?	Gen. 11:1 words		Acts 2:8, 46 the Word	
What was raised up?	Gen. 11:4		Psa. 18:2; Acts 2:22-24	
What materials were used?	Gen. 11:3		1 Pet. 2:5-6	
Where did they seek to live?	Gen. 11:4		Heb. 12:22-23	
What did they seek for themselves?	Gen. 11:4		Isa. 62:2; Acts 11:26	
What was their goal?	Gen. 11:4		2 Cor. 5:1-2	
What did God do?	Gen. 11:7		Acts 2:6-8	
The was the outcome?	Gen. 11:8		Acts 8:1, 4	

*The LORD is my rock, and my fortress, and my deliverer; my God, my
strength, in whom I will trust; my buckler, and the horn of my
salvation, and my high tower.*
- Psalm 18:2 (KJV)

Building in Vain

Ken Gehrels of Ontario, Canada once wrote a piece about the story of Babel. He wrote: "It's a brief, but all too clear story, told in the same pithy, condensed form as the account of creation. Humanity gathers. Their sense of self-worth knows no bounds. Sky's the limit, it seems. Build a tower and extend human influence right to the gates of heaven. Behave as gods."

The story of Babel reveals in many ways what happens when mankind becomes egocentric. God has issued a command to "fill the earth" (Gen. 9:1, 7) but man has a different idea and a different plan. Their plan is to stick together and to reach for heaven on their own terms. It's the human condition in a microcosm. Is it any different today? We erect monuments to ourselves and become gods in our own eyes. The events of Babel tell us about our own lust for power and our selfishness. God-seeking takes a variety of forms as different religions seek to find God on their own terms rather than His.

Is it wrong to be speak the same language? Is it wrong to seek God? Is it wrong to want to attain heaven? Not at all! But God has His own plan for accomplishing those things. The blueprints have been drawn and we need to follow His direction and design all of which are revealed in Acts 2. The day of Pentecost is Babel in reverse. A common language, a spirit of unity, and the means of attaining heaven have all been found....in Christ alone.

Unless the LORD builds the house,
the builders labor in vain.
Unless the LORD watches over the city,
the guards stand watch in vain.
- Psalm 127:1

For Discussion: Is the Babel "story" purposefully related to the events that unfolded on the day of Pentecost, or are the comparisons mere coincidence?

NOTE: The passage on the front page of this lesson is Genesis 11:7-9 translated into Esperanto.

CHRIST FORESHADOWED IN TWO MEN OF FAITH

JOSEPH & MOSES

Have you ever risen early to read your Bible and as you sip a morning cup of coffee or tea you suddenly "see" for the first time an amazing parallel between an Old Testament "story" and the Son of God? It's often happened to me and it's like blinders have been removed as the threads of the story stretch forward and reveal a tapestry that is Christ.

Take Abraham for instance. We read of his humble journey of faith as he did the bidding of God and travelled from Ur to Haran and then on to Canaan – the land of promise. Similarly, Christ journeyed from heaven to earth at the bidding of His Father. It was Abraham who became the focal point of a new generation and a new nation founded on a covenant with God and on God's promises. So too did Christ.

Journey of Abraham

Then, there is the name "Abram" which means "the honored father." His name is later changed to "Abraham" which means "father of many nations" all pointing to the future when all nations – Jew and Gentile – who have the same faith as Abraham, might become children of God through Christ (Gen. 17:5, John 8:39).

The story of Abraham as a type, and indeed all the types and shadows of the Old Testament, was purposefully revealed by God for us to learn of Christ and of His church. Old Testament types were "anticipations" or "pictures" of Jesus and His atoning work that by them we may learn of Jesus the Savior.

In this lesson we will focus attention on two great men of faith whose lives are revealed in the Old Testament and who were "types" of Jesus: Joseph and Moses.

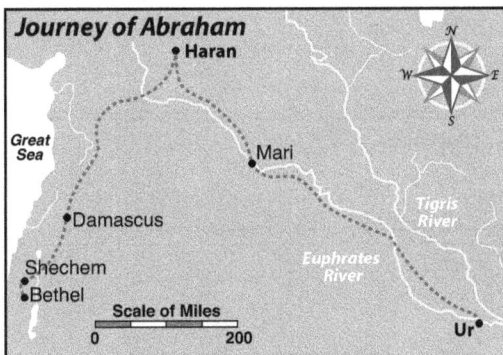

For Study and Discussion

1. Joseph seems to have been a "type" of Jesus in many ways. In the boxes below indicate ways Joseph's life foreshadowed the life of Jesus.

Joseph

In Joseph's character and experience we have a wonderful type of our Lord Jesus Christ. His life shines forth from the pages of Holy Scripture as practically flawless. It is not indeed that he was actually sinless, for he certainly sinned, but it did not please God to speak of any flaws of blemishes which His holy eye may have discerned in this devoted servant, but He has rather emphasized his faithfulness and practical godliness.
— H. A. Ironside

Joseph... Gen. 37:3	Christ... Matt. 3:17
...was the beloved son of Jacob	...is the beloved Son of God
Joseph...	Christ...
Joseph...	Christ...
Joseph...	Christ...
Joseph...	Christ...
Joseph...	Christ...

2. Of whom might the following be said?

He was despised and rejected, hated and spurned, and given up for dead; but was resurrected that he might give life, and that abundantly.

3. God told Moses He would raise up a prophet like him (Deut. 18:15, 18). The promise was fulfilled in Christ according to Acts 3:21-23. List below some of the ways Moses' life and work were a "type" of Christ.

Moses... Exod. 1:22	Christ.. Matt. 2:16
...was preserved as an infant from Pharaoh's edict.	...was preserved as an infant from Herod's edict.
Moses...	Christ...
Moses...	Christ...
Moses...	Christ...
Moses...	Christ...
Moses...	Christ...

Moses

4. Abraham, Joseph, and Moses – each in his own way – were "types" of Jesus Christ. Interestingly, those same three men of the Old Testament are mentioned by Stephen in the sermon he preached just before his death (Acts 7). What was Stephen's point in mentioning these three?

The life of Moses presents a series of striking antitheses....He was a fugitive from Pharaoh, and an ambassador from heaven. He was the giver of the Law, and the forerunner of grace. He died alone on Mount Moab, and appeared with Christ in the mount of transfiguration. No man assisted at his funeral, yet God buried him. His lips are silent, but his voice yet speaks.
- Dr. I. M. Haldeman

The Glorious Tapestry of Christ

According to Hank Hanegraaff, Biblical typology, as evidenced in the writings of the New Testament, always "involves a heightening of the type (the Old Testament person, event or ceremony) in the antitype" (Jesus Christ or His church). In other words, according to Hanegraaff "it is not simply that Jesus *replaces* the temple as a new but otherwise equal substitute. No, Jesus is far greater than the temple." The Bible student, then, should not see Jesus as simply another great man in the line of great men. No, Jesus is far superior to even the greatest of the great men of the Old Testament. This is confirmed on the mount of transfiguration when Jesus is declared by God Himself to be far superior to Moses the great lawgiver, and Elijah the great prophet (Matt. 17:1-5). The new covenant, then, is not equal to the old. It is superior. The new covenant not only replaces the old but eclipses it (Heb. 8:13).

Just as Joshua is a type of Jesus who leads the children of Israel into the land of promise, so King David is an inferior type of Jesus who is the "King of kings and Lord of lords" ruling and reigning forever in a spiritual kingdom. So while the stories of the great men of faith found in the Old Testament lead us to Christ, they are all inferior to Him.

As we study the Old Testament, then, we should anticipate in the many great men of faith the coming superiority of Jesus. The great men of old – prophets, priests, and kings – all, in some aspect of their lives, foreshadowed the coming Messiah but they were mere threads in the grand and glorious tapestry Who is Jesus the Redeemer.

– "What Is the Significance of Biblical Typology?" by Hank Hanegraaff, December 20, 2011, Christian Research Institute.

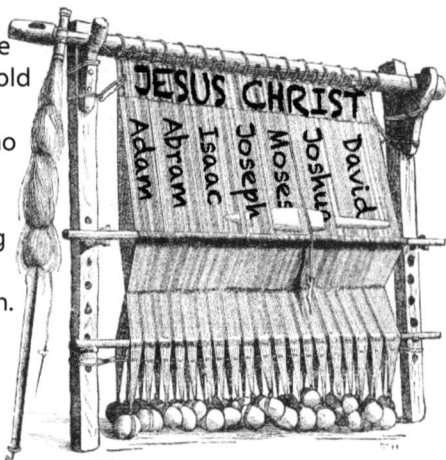

For Discussion: Was Christ also foreshadowed in women of faith? If so, what women of faith in Old Testament were "types" for Jesus Christ or of his redemptive work? Be prepared to share points of comparison and similarities.

THE CONSTANT THREAT OF SATAN AND SIN

TYPES & SHADOWS

THE AMALEKITES

The Amalekites were a biblical people and ongoing enemy of the Israelites who fought against them regularly soon after their departure from Egyptian bondage all the way into the period of captivity recorded late in the Old Testament record. Amalekite settlements are reported in the biblical record as late as the reign of King Hezekiah in the eighth century B.C. and ancestors of the Amalekite people continued to trouble God's people even into the days of Queen Esther.

According to most reference sources the Amalekites are unknown historically and archaeologically outside of the Bible record except for traditions which themselves seem to have relied on biblical accounts. Of course, we, who believe and accept the Bible's historical record, will recall that the Amalekites were descended from a common ancestor named "Amalek" (Gen. 36:12).

Because the Amalekites frequently attacked God's people, the Bible and Jewish tradition both paint them as a relentless, evil enemy of God and Israel. To many, the Amalekites have come to represent the *archetypal* enemy of the Jews.

The hasidic teacher Baal Shem Tov (circa 1700 - 1760) used the term "Amalekite" to represent the total rejection of God, or atheism, and the term has been used metaphorically throughout history to refer to enemies of Judaism. Such was the case in 1962 when Israeli President Itzhak Ben-Zvi turned down Nazi war criminal Adolf Eichmann's petition for mercy before his execution. Ben-Zvi quoted Samuel's words to King Agag who had briefly survived Saul's war on the Amalekites: *"As your sword bereaved women, so will your mother be bereaved among women"* (1 Sam. 15:33).

Aaron and Hur hold up Moses' hands to secure victory against the Amalekites (Exod. 17:8-16).

For Study and Discussion

1. For approximately how many years did God's people have problems with the Amalekites? (**Hint:** They are first mentioned in Exodus 17 and the final reference to an Amalekite is in Esther 7.)

2. Of whom were the Amalekites offspring (Gen. 36:12)? What does the Bible tell us about this person (Heb. 12:16)?

3. What method of attack was used by the Amalekites at Rephidim? (Deut. 25:17-19.)

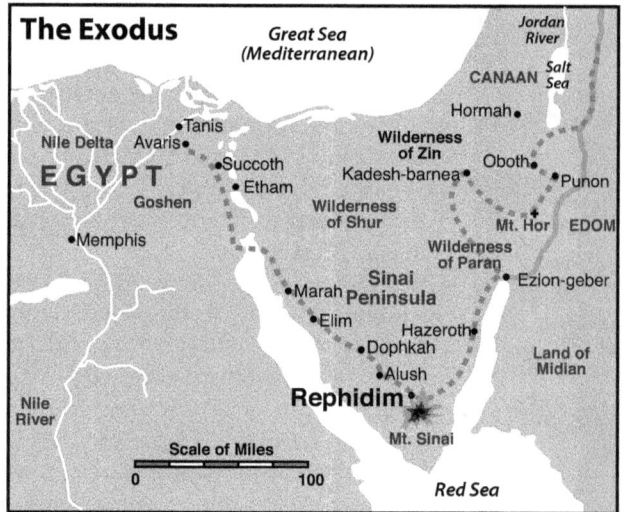

The Exodus

Great Sea (Mediterranean)

Jordan River

CANAAN *Salt Sea*

Hormah•

•Tanis

Nile Delta Avaris•

Wilderness of Zin

Oboth•

EGYPT

•Succoth

Kadesh-barnea•

•Punon

• Etham

Goshen

Wilderness of Shur

Mt. Hor EDOM

•Memphis

Wilderness of Paran

Sinai Peninsula

•Marah

• Ezion-geber

•Elim

Hazeroth•

•Dophkah

Land of Midian

•Alush

Nile River

Rephidim•

Mt. Sinai

Scale of Miles

0   100

Red Sea

4. Read 1 Samuel 15:1-26. What was Saul's motivation for preserving the Amalekite flocks? What notable figure escaped death – at least for a time? What is meant by the word "good" in 1 Samuel 15:9?

5. Read 2 Samuel 1:1-10, 14-16. What is ironic about the events in these verses? What did the Amalekite take from Saul and give to David?

6. Read Esther 3:1-6 and answer the following questions:

Why did Mordecai refuse to bow to Haman? Is bowing to men forbidden?

Why was Haman so angry with Mordecai?

What did Haman decide to do to *all* the Jews? Did his decision seem a bit excessive?

7. Review your answers to questions 1- 6 and complete the left side of the chart below. The right side of the chart will be completed in class:

The Amalekites	Satan and Sin
They were an ever present, constant threat. **Exod. 17:16**	
What attack strategy did they use at Rephidim? **Deut. 25:17-19**	
How did Saul view the spoil of battle? **1 Sam. 15:9**	
What did an Amalekite claim to do to Saul? **2 Sam. 1:10**	
What did the Amalekite take from Saul's head? **2 Sam. 1:10**	
Whom did Haman hate? What was his intent? **Est. 3:1-6**	

Sin Masquerades As Good

Sadly, we live in a relativistic world wherein the lines are often blurred between good and evil. What I view as evil, others view as good. What I view as good, others view as evil. This should come as no surprise because Isaiah the prophet lived in such a time and denounced this inclination of men: *"Woe unto them that call evil good, and good evil; that put darkness for light, and light for darkness; that put bitter for sweet, and sweet for bitter!"* (Isa. 5:20)

Paul Tripp in an article entitled "As You Are" (*The Gospel Coalition*, December 5, 2011) wrote that "sin lives in a costume." He went on to say that "in order for sin to do its evil work it must present itself as something that is anything but evil." If we are honest with ourselves we can only concur with his assessment. In our own lives we often see our flaws and our sins in a better light than they deserve. Behaviors denounced by God's Word are oftened seen as "good." Need proof? Witness how our world sees "alternative lifestyles" as good and even praiseworthy despite the clear denunciations of such in God's Word. King Saul had the same problem. Despite God's clear command, Saul saw "good" in that which was in violation of God's clear command (1 Sam. 15:3, 9).

In continuing his assertion that sin masquerades as good, Tripp continues: "An impatient moment of yelling wears the costume of zeal for truth. Lust masquerades as a love for beauty. Gossip lives in the costume of concern and prayer. Craving for power and control wears the mask of biblical leadership."

The challenge we all face is seeing ourselves for what we are: sinners in need of redemption. Our constant ambition should be to see ourselves as God sees us – to behold our face in the mirror of the Word (Jam. 1:23-24). Satan is clever, so sin will always look good unless we allow the Word of God to open our eyes.

For Discussion: Are the Old Testament events involving the Amalekites meant to be a "type" of Satan and sin and the threat they pose to us today, or are these similarities just interesting parallels or mere coincidence?

CHRIST IN THE WILDERNESS

A SPIRITUAL ROCK

CHRIST

As we noted in our last lesson, the Amalekites, while perhaps not a "type" in the usual sense of the word, do represent a compelling *parallel* to the threat posed by Satan and sin. Just as the Amalekites were a constant threat to God's people, so too is Satan a constant threat to us.

Good and evil were at odds right from the beginning in the Garden of Eden, and as God's plan for saving mankind unfolds in the pages of the Old Testament the ongoing clash between God and Satan is always center stage. God is good. Satan is the destroyer of all that is good, and he is seeking to destroy us. Peter captured the essence of Satan, as a destroyer, when he warned in 1 Peter 5:8, *"be of sober spirit, be on the alert. Your adversary, the devil, prowls around like a roaring lion, seeking someone to devour."*

Thankfully, God's great love for us does not leave us wondering how to successfully defend ourselves against Satan and his wiles. Even in that first of many skirmishes between God's people and the Amalekites there are some compelling insights about how we can prepare ourselves to deal with Satan and sin and be victorious over him.

As an introduction to this lesson, review how God's people were able to win the victory against the Amalekites at Rephidim. Pay close attention to Exodus 17:11-12 and the specific steps taken to ensure God's people prevailed against the Amalekites. Do the verses provide any clues about how we might win our own battles with the evil one? Here's a hint: a childhood song provides a clue about one of the most frequently used "types" found in the Old Testament:

The wise man built his house upon the rock.
The wise man built his house upon the rock.
The wise man built his house upon the rock,
And the rain came tumbling down....

So, build your house on the Lord Jesus Christ.
Build your house on the Lord Jesus Christ.
Build your house on the Lord Jesus Christ,
And the blessings will come down.

For Study and Discussion

1. What role did Moses' hands play in the battle with the Amalekites (Exod. 17:11)? What connection is there between Moses' supplicant posture and how we can be victorious against Satan and sin (1 Tim. 2:8; Heb. 5:7; James. 5:15)?

2. What action do Aaron and Hur take to ensure victory for the Lord's people in their battle with the Amalekites? What lessons are there for us in what they did (Gal. 6:2; 1 Thess. 5:11; Heb. 3:13)?

3. As we noted, while the "stone" of Exodus 17:12 may not have much "typical" significance, what is the significance in the "stone" mentioned in Romans 9:33 and 1 Peter 2:7-9? Who is the "stone" of these passages?

4. What did Samuel do to Agag, the king of the Amalekites? What lesson might this provide us about our attitude toward sin?

Our problem with sin is that we like to keep it right nearby and accessible, rather than getting as far from it as possible.

Shouldn't our response to sin be the same as Samuel's response to King Agag?
1 Samuel 15:33

5. Earlier in the chapter of the story of the Amalekites we read of a rock (Exod. 17:1-7). According to 1 Corinthians 10:1-6 who is the rock from which Israel received life-giving water?

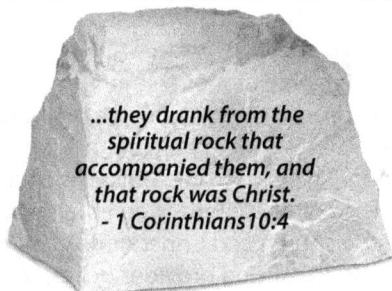

6. In what ways might the rock of Exodus 17 be comparable to Christ? List as many similarities as you can think of below:

...they drank from the spiritual rock that accompanied them, and that rock was Christ.
- 1 Corinthians 10:4

The Type	*The Antitype*
The rock was...	*Similarly, Christ is...*
The rock was...	*Similarly, Christ is...*
The rock was...	*Similarly, Christ is...*
The rock was...	*Similarly, Christ is...*
The rock was...	*Similarly, Christ is...*
The rock was...	*Similarly, Christ is...*

7. How do the following verses relate to the water from the rock events of Exodus 17?

• John 4:7-14

• Matt. 7:24

• Matt. 16:18

The Rock of Matthew 16:18

Jesus often used wordplay to make a point. For instance, in Matthew 16:18 in a spiritual discussion with Peter, Jesus used Peter's Greek name *petros* (a small pebble or movable stone) in contrast to *petra* (a bedrock or immovable foundation) to differentiate between Peter's faith (a pebble) and the bedrock upon which He would build His church.

The connection between the "rock" foundation of the church and Christ Himself is compelling. The Word of God provides dozens of instances of Christ or His church being referred to as a rock or a stone. Note for instance the following:

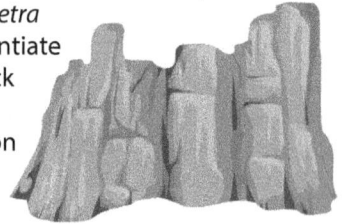

> *Now therefore ye are no more strangers and foreigners, but fellow citizens with the saints, and of the household of God; And are built upon the foundation of the apostles and prophets, Jesus Christ himself being the chief cornerstone.* - Ephesians 2:19-20

> *Moreover, brethren, I would not that ye should be ignorant, how that all our fathers were under the cloud, and all passed through the sea; and were all baptized unto Moses in the cloud and in the sea; and did all eat the same spiritual meat; and did all drink the same spiritual drink: for they drank of that spiritual Rock that followed them: and that Rock was Christ.* - 1 Corinthians 10:1-4

As we study the Old Testament we should be watching for Christ revealed in its pages. References to a rock or a stone may signal a "type," and in so doing help us learn more about the coming Messiah and the firm, spiritual foundation to be found in Him.

For Discussion: The Bible makes it clear the rock which brought forth life-giving water in Exodus 17:6 was Christ, but what of the rock of Numbers 20:8-12? Is that the same "type" of Christ, and what are we to make of Moses' disobedience in *striking* the rock rather than *speaking* to it? Why was God so angry?

THE DWELLING PLACE OF GOD

THE TABERNACLE

The tabernacle – the sacred, portable place of worship built by God's people soon after their departure from Egypt – is rather mysterious and raises many questions about the ceremonies and rites performed in it. Despite the many questions, however, there is no doubt the structure and its furnishings are "types" foreshadowing Christ and the church.

The importance of the tabernacle is seen not only in the specific details provided about it but also in the sheer number of Bible chapters devoted to its construction and transport. In this regard, Brevard S. Childs in *The Book of Exodus* said, *"God created the whole world in six days, but he used forty to instruct Moses about the tabernacle. Little over one chapter was needed to describe the structure of the world, but six were used for the tabernacle."* It is mentioned in fifty Bible chapters.

The tabernacle was built by the children of Israel under the supervision of Moses, around 1450 B.C. The structure is known in Hebrew as the *mishkan. Mishkan* is related to the Hebrew word to "dwell," "rest," or "to live in," referring to the "in-dwelling Presence of God."

The tabernacle consisted of a tent-like structure covered by rug-like coverings for a roof, and an external courtyard (150 feet by 75 feet). The whole compound was surrounded by a fence about 7 feet high. The tent was divided into the Holy Place and the Holy of Holies and was built of acacia wood boards overlaid with gold and fitted together to form the walls. Six pieces of furniture were built and placed in the structure, two in the courtyard, three in the Holy Place, and one in the Holy of Holies.

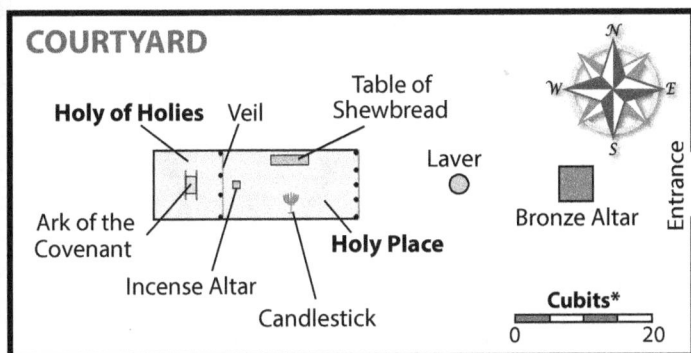

COURTYARD

Holy of Holies   Veil

Table of Shewbread

Laver

Ark of the Covenant

Incense Altar

Candlestick

Holy Place

Bronze Altar

Entrance

Cubits*
0   20

*A royal cubit was approximately 18 inches.

THE TABERNACLE

One can scarcely contemplate the peculiar structure of the tabernacle with its various apartments, its strange furniture, its bloody sacrifices, and its mysterious rites without being impressed with the fact that it must be of symbolic significance, even if the Scriptures were silent as to the fact. We need have no doubt the tabernacle was a type. – D.S. Warner

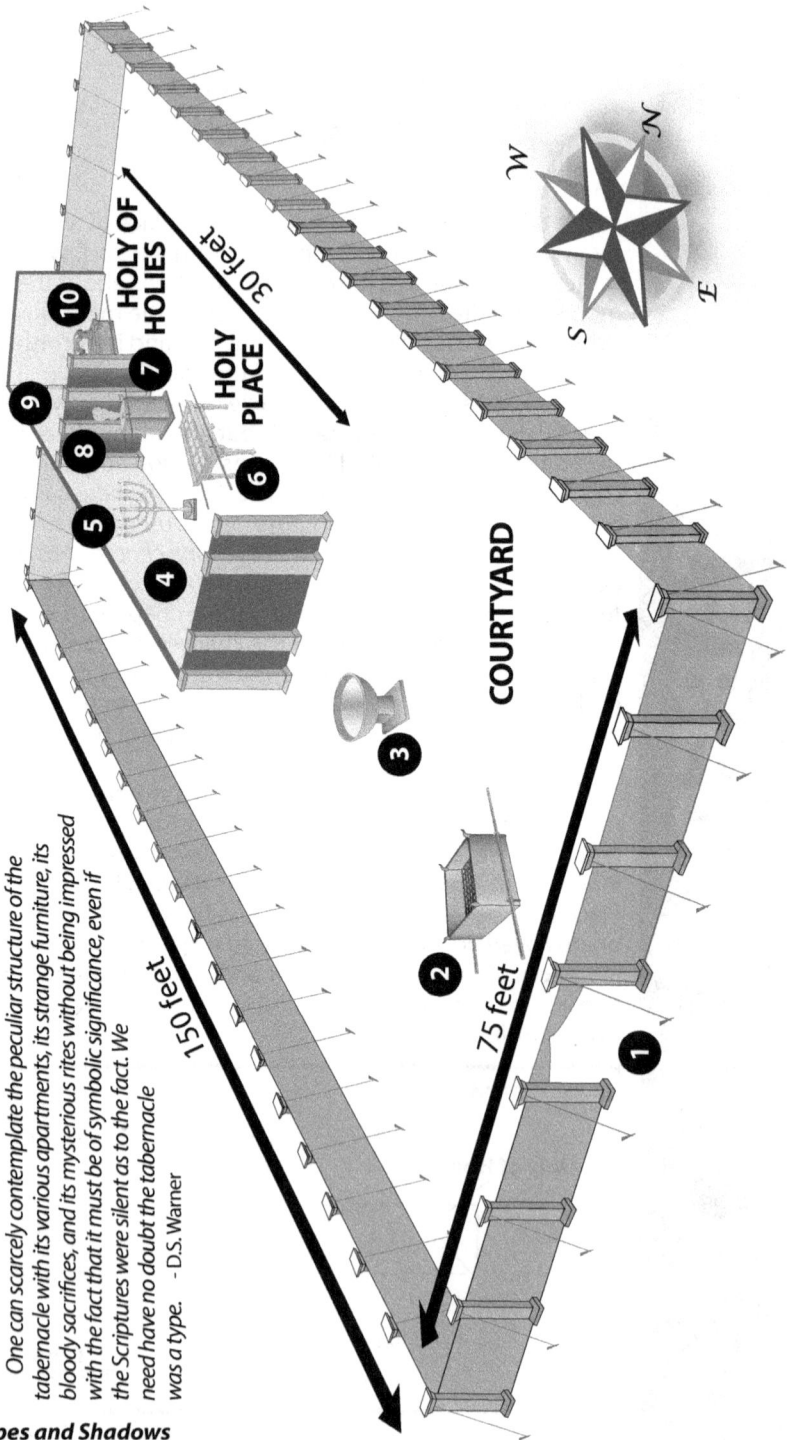

HOLY OF HOLIES

HOLY PLACE

COURTYARD

150 feet

75 feet

30 feet

For Study and Discussion

1. By what other names was the tabernacle known? List at least three. What is the meaning conveyed by each?

2. Read Hebrews 8:1-2; 9:1-28; and 10:19-22. What does the Hebrew writer say about the tabernacle by way of comparison?

3. In what ways is Jesus, according to the Hebrew writer, associated with the tabernacle?

4. Since the Bible explicitly tells us the tabernacle is a "figure" and a "shadow," what does it foreshadow? What is the reality to which it points?

5. Is the tabernacle in its entirety a type or are each of its features and pieces of furniture types? If each is a type, what might each foreshadow?

1	*The Entrance*
2	*The Brazen Altar*
3	*The Laver*
4	*The Holy Place*
5	*The Lampstand*
6	*The Table of Shewbread*
7	*The Altar of Incense*
8	*The Veil*
9	*The Holy of Holies*

10 **NOTE:** *We will consider #10, the ark of the covenant, in our next lesson.*

THE BLEST PAVILION

There is a blest pavilion,
A sacred inner court,
The place of God's own dwelling,
With all the world shut out.
Oh, holy resting place!
Oh, calm and pure retreat!
Where God unveils his face,
And life is only sweet.

Within this greater temple,
Built by the Son of God,
We've found a full salvation,
And entered thro' the blood.
Here on the mercy seat,
Beneath the cherubim,
We dwell in love complete,
And heaven's glory hymn.

First at the cleansing laver
We felt the blood applied,
Then on the golden altar
We're wholly sanctified.
Within the second veil,
Oh, holy, holy, place!
With joyful lips we tell
The fullness of his grace.

Oh, glory be to Jesus!
I've boldly entered in
The secret of his presence,
and triumph over sin.
My soul is hid away
In God, with Jesus Christ;
And here I'll ever stay,
In sweet eternal rest.

– D. S. Warner 1842 - 1895

_____

For Discussion: The tabernacle compound had three separate entrances, each leading to a more sacred spot:

1. The entrance to the courtyard
2. The entrance to the Holy Place
3. The entrance to the Holy of Holies

What might these three entrances represent?

Who was allowed to enter the Holy Place?

Who was allowed to enter the Holy of Holies?

WORSHIP
TYPES & SHADOWS

ARK OF THE COVENANT

What most people *think* they know about the Ark of the Covenant comes from the 1981 release of *Raiders of the Lost Ark*. The American action-adventure film directed by Steven Spielberg pits Indiana Jones against a group of Nazis who are searching for the Ark of the Covenant which Adolf Hitler believes will give his army supernatural powers. As one would expect, the movie departs from reality in a number of ways. Contrary to Spielberg's fictional story, the Ark had no innate power, indeed it was ineffectual in preventing Israel's defeat by the Philistines who themselves took possession of the Ark (1 Sam. 4).

What the Bible tells us is that the Ark was a box 3 feet 9 inches in length, by 2 feet 3 inches in height, by 2 feet 3 inches in width (a cubit was approximately18 inches). It was constructed of acacia wood, and was covered with pure gold, inside and out. On the bottom of the box, four gold rings were attached, through which two poles, made of acacia and coated in gold, were placed. The family of Kohath, of the tribe of Levi, carried the Ark.

The Ark disappeared from biblical history after King Solomon with only a few passing references. In 2 Chronicles 35:3, the Levites were told by King Josiah not to carry the Ark any longer. Later, during the return from captivity the prophet Jeremiah (3:16) said the Ark would not be remembered or replaced, because Jerusalem would be the "Throne of the Lord." In the new temple – about which Ezekiel prophesied – the Ark is not mentioned because in the new kingdom God will no longer be a God dwelling symbolically between the cherubim of the Ark, but will be a God ruling all nations from heaven with a new covenant.

There are many legends about the present day location of the Ark. Some say the Ark sits in a cave beneath the Temple Mount, while others place it in a cave on Mt. Nebo. Others speculate the Ark is in Egypt or Ethiopia. Revelation 11:19 suggests the Ark has symbolically returned to the direct care of God.

For Study and Discussion

In the last lesson we dealt with many of the types and shadows associated with the tabernacle and most of its furnishings. In this lesson we will consider in some detail the Ark of the Covenant and take another look at the lampstand and the possible association it might have to the Lord's church. Additionally we will focus on two of the animal sacrifices offered in worship under the old law to see what "typical" significance they may have.

The Lampstand

In what ways might a lampstand be comparable to a local church? Consider Exodus 25:1-40; Luke 11:33; Philippians 2:14-16; and Revelation 1:12-13, 20.

1

"...and the seven golden lampstands are the seven churches." - Revelation 1:20

The Paschal Lamb

What are the characteristics of lambs or sheep that are comparable to Christ? Is Christ the Passover or is He the lamb? Consider Exodus 12:3-14; Numbers 9:12; John 1:29, 36; 19:32-33; and 1 Corinthians 5:7.

2

The Ark of the Covenant

In what ways is Christ like the lid of the ark of the covenant? What was inside the ark? Is there any significance to those items? Consider Exodus 25:10-22; Numbers 10:32-34; and Hebrews 9:3-5.

3

God "dwelt" between the cherubim (Isa. 37:14-16).

The "mercy seat" or "cover" of the ark.

The Scapegoat

There were two goats used in the Day of Atonement offering. Which one does Christ represent? Could Judas be the "special" or "fit" man who led the scapegoat (Jesus) into the wilderness? Consider Leviticus 16:6-10, 20-22; John 1:29; Matthew 4:1-11; Hebrews 9:28; and 1 Peter 2:24.

4

Jewish history records that it was a common practice to tie a red strip of cloth to the scapegoat. The red strip represented the sin of the people which was atoned for by the red blood on the mercy seat. According to the Jewish Talmud this red strip would eventually turn white, signaling God's acceptance of the offering.

- Talmud, Rosh HaShanah 31b, & Bavli, Yoma 39b

A Quest to Find the Ark of the Covenant
Searching for What Has Already Been Found

One of the most mysterious and awesome objects found in the Old Testament is the Ark of the Covenant. As we have noted, movies have been made that embellish what we learn in the Bible about the Ark, and much mystery surrounds its construction and use. A question that often occurs to Bible students is this: "Where is the Ark today?"

The last Old Testament reference to the Ark of the Covenant reveals it was in the Temple in Jerusalem. We are told King Hezekiah *"...prayed to the Lord, saying: 'O Lord of hosts, God of Israel, the One who dwells between the cherubim'"* (Isa. 37:14-16). This reference to God dwelling between the cherubim confirms the Ark was still located in the Holy of Holies of the Temple about 701 B.C.

What became of the Ark and its current location (if it still exists) has been the subject of great conjecture and speculation. It was likely carried away into captivity as plunder. No doubt intrepid archeologists have attempted to find clues to the Ark's current location with the goal of finding it.

For the child of God, the quest to find the Ark is already over. Those who search to find the *physical* Ark fail to realize the real treasure is in the *spiritual* riches of the new covenant the Ark foreshadowed.

Jim May in a sermon entitled "Ark of the Covenant" (*sermoncentral.com*) made this point: *"...the covenant of God and the spiritual riches it provides are available right now for the taking. It's there in the Word of God. It's there in the sacrifice of Jesus upon the cross. It's there in the heart of every man and woman born as a child of God.... The new covenant in Christ can give eternal life, and is far more valuable than any wooden box overlaid with gold."*

FOR DISCUSSION: According to Catholic teaching, the Ark of the Covenant is a "type" and Mary, the mother of Jesus, is the "antitype." The conclusion they reach then is that since Mary is the Ark of the New Covenant, she is the most sacred person on earth other than Jesus Christ himself. What are your thoughts about this?

THE HORROR OF SIN

LOATHSOME LEPROSY

The description of leprosy provided in Leviticus 13 and 14 is said to be one of the oldest if not the oldest description of any disease found in a written record. The biblical description was not given, however, for medical purposes, nor were the regulations concerning it for effecting a cure. Instead the Bible's intructions were given for diagnosis and then later, when a sufferer was found to be free of the disease, the specific steps to be taken so the leper could be declared clean.

Leprosy is an infectious disease that causes severe, disfiguring skin sores and nerve damage in the arms and legs. The disease has been prevalent since ancient times, often resulting in terrifying, negative stigmas. In many ancient cultures leprosy sufferers were shunned as outcasts. Outbreaks of leprosy have affected and frightened people of every culture on every continent.

Leprosy primarily affects the skin and the nerves outside the brain and spinal cord called the peripheral nerves. It also affects the eyes and the thin tissue lining the inside of the nose.

The main symptom of leprosy is disfiguring skin lesions, lumps, or protrusions that persist for several weeks or years. The skin sores are pale-colored. Nerve damage associated with the disease can lead to a loss of feeling in the arms and legs and overall muscle weakness. The time between contact with the bacteria that causes leprosy and the appearance of symptoms can be months or years. Leprosy's long incubation period makes it very difficult for doctors to determine when and where a person with leprosy got infected.

For the Bible student it is interesting to note that while there were many ailments and diseases present in biblical times, none get the attention that leprosy does. Why is leprosy dealt with in such detail in the Bible record? Could it be that leprosy is a type? If so, what is the antitype?

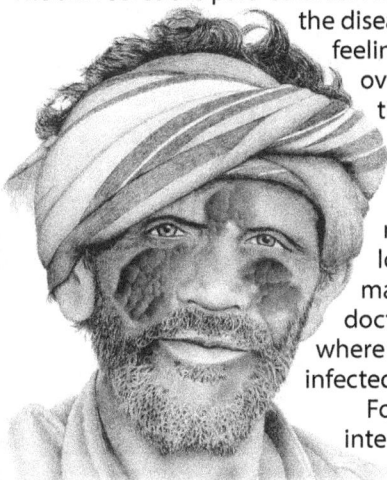

For Study and Discussion

1. Who was given the responsibility for diagnosing skin diseases, in particular leprosy?

2. If one were found to have leprosy, some very specific things were to happen to him. Read Leviticus 13:45-46 and list the actions below:

1. _____
2. _____
3. _____
4. _____
5. _____
6. _____

3. According to Leviticus 14: 4, 10 what animals were used to cleanse the one who had been afflicted with leprosy? Why do you think so many animals were involved in the cleansing ceremony?

4. Other than the birds, what other items were used in the cleansing process? How might these items relate to our own cleansing from sin?

5. What animal was freed as part of the ceremony? What might this symbolize? (See Psa. 124:7-8.)

6. How is leprosy like sin? List below all the similarities that occur to you:

| |
| |
| |
| |
| |
| |

7. What instructions did Elisha give Naaman as the cure for his leprosy (2 Kings 5)?

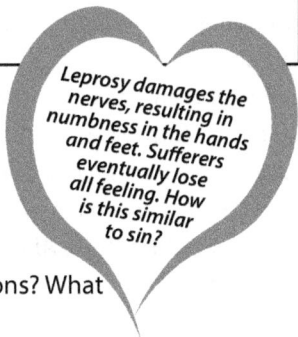

Leprosy damages the nerves, resulting in numbness in the hands and feet. Sufferers eventually lose all feeling. How is this similar to sin?

8. What was Naaman's reaction to Elisha's instructions? What alternative cure did Naaman prefer?

9. What was accomplished when Naaman finally did as Elisha instructed?

10. Who did the work of cleansing Naaman? Did Naaman have to do anything for the cleansing to be accomplished? Explain.

11. Was Naaman's leprosy and cure a "shadow" or a "type" for anything later revealed in the New Testament? If so, what? Be specific and provide supporting Scriptures.

How Is Leprosy Like Sin?

While leprosy has largely been cured in the modern world, during Old and New Testament times the disease was without parallel in evoking fear and revulsion. Lepers, who stumbled about with toeless feet and oozing sores, were viewed as the "walking dead" and were shunned by society.

The Bible tells us the disease was so onerous that anyone who contracted it was to have his *"clothes torn, the hair of his head uncovered, and must cover his mustache and cry, 'Unclean! Unclean'"* (Lev. 13:45)!

John Barnett, in an article entitled "Touched by Jesus" (*Discover the Book Ministries*), wrote, "Leprosy is a vivid and graphic physical picture of the spiritual defilement of sin. Sin is ugly, loathsome, incurable, and contaminating; it separates men from God and makes them outcasts." Leprosy also causes numbness and eventually all loss of feeling. Does that not sound like sin?

Fortunately, Jesus has the power to cure leprosy. Note for instance Matthew 8:2-3: *"...behold, a leper came to him and knelt before him, saying, 'Lord, if you will, you can make me clean.' And Jesus stretched out his hand and touched him, saying, 'I will; be clean.' And immediately his leprosy was cleansed."*

More importantly, Jesus has the power to cure sin! By His blood, by His touch, we who are disfigured by sin can be healed!

———————————————————

FOR DISCUSSION: Is leprosy a type of sin, or just an interesting parallel?

RAHAB IN REHAB

SALVATION IN JERICHO

Have you ever written someone off as so bad, so evil, that in your eyes he is beyond God's reach? All of us at times are quick to judge others by their looks, their behavior, or their past. Then we conclude such persons would never accept the teaching of Christ, His grace or His love. Such a conclusion is wrong! A study of the Word of God reveals example after example of God's willingness to welcome even the vilest of sinners. What is repeatedly shown in Scripture is that God is good at *rehabilitation* and *reconciliation*. No one is too far gone or too distant from His love. God doesn't write anyone off.

Rahab – forever remembered as a harlot – was a woman who seemingly had nothing going for her. She was a prostitute dwelling in Jericho that lay in the path of destruction as God's fledgling nation assembled just to the east. The city was known for its worship of idols, in particular the Ashtaroth – the goddess of the moon. Jericho represented all that was sinful and degrading in the promised land and in many ways *typifies* the world in which we live. However, despite her sinful occupation and the fact that she lived amongst sinful, godless people, Rahab found salvation.

The story of Rahab recounted in Joshua chapters 2 and 6 is a story about breaking down walls – yes, physical walls – but also spiritual walls. The story of Rahab and her household reveals that any one of the inhabitants of Jericho who wanted salvation could have had it, but only one woman and her family were willing to break down the walls of self will and submit to the conditions of salvation.

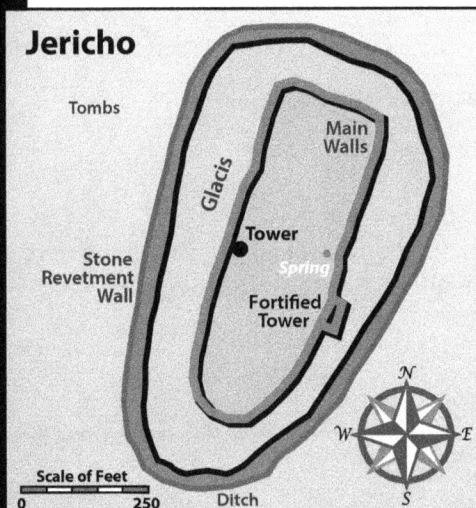

Why is the story of Rahab included in the biblical record? Is it there as just some kind of human interest story or are there more important lessons to be learned? Are the events recounted meant as a type and if so what is the antitype?

Jericho

Tombs

Main Walls

Glacis

Tower

Spring

Stone Revetment Wall

Fortified Tower

Scale of Feet
0   250

Ditch

N E S W

For Study and Discussion

1. What had Rahab and the inhabitants of Jericho heard about God's people, Israel? How did this knowledge affect the people of the city?

2. Much debate exists about Rahab's occupation. Was she really a a prostitute or merely an inn-keeper* as some surmise? Explain.

3. What does James have to say about Rahab (James 2:25)? For what, specifically, is she praised? Was it right for her to lie to those seeking the spies? Explain.

4. What was Rahab's declaration of faith?

5. What request did Rahab make of the spies?

6. List below the specific conditions required of Rahab if she were to survive the coming destruction of Jericho:

* The New International Version translators attached a marginal note to the word "prostitute" in Joshua 2:1 that reads, "Or possibly an innkeeper."

7. List below possible "shadows" or "types" of the plan of salvation as revealed in the story of Rahab and her family. Consider the Bible passages provided.

1 What was Rahab's **CONDITION** as God's armies drew near?
Isa. 59:2; Rom. 3:10-23; 6:23

2 What was Rahab's **CONDUCT** that prepared her for salvation?
Heb. 11:31; James 2:25

3 What did Rahab **CONFESS** about the Lord and His works?
Rom. 14:11; 2 Tim. 2:19; 1 John 1:9

Is there anything significant about the scarlet cord that marked the house of those to be spared in the attack? To what Bible event does this seem similar?

4 How was Rahab **CONSECRATED** from the doomed?
2 Tim. 1:9; 2:20-22; Heb. 12:14; 1 Pet. 2:9

5 What **COMPANY** did Rehab keep after Jericho's destruction?
Eph. 2:11-13, 19; 3:6; 1 Tim. 3:15

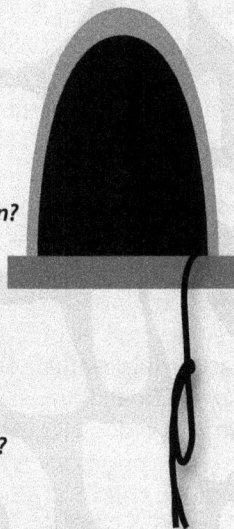

By faith Rahab the harlot did not perish along with those who were disobedient....
- Hebrews 11:31

The Scarlet Cord

Most of the people we read about in the Bible have serious character flaws. From start to end we read about liars, cheaters, adulterers, and murderers. We are introduced to a king who *"sacrificed his own son in the fire"* (2 Kings 21:6) yet repented and found forgiveness from God (2 Chron. 33). Then, of course, there's Rahab the hartlot.

Think for a moment about all these tainted people. Now imagine interviewing them for a job: you'd take one look at their résumés and quickly reject them. Nope, can't use you. Sorry, you aren't qualified. God, however, seems to relish telling us about some of the worst people through the ages who were transformed by Him and found salvation. Frankly, most of the salvation stories of the Bible are amazing and dumbfounding. But, if we are honest, we soon realize our stories are the same: all of us have cheated, all of us have lied, all of us have had terrible, sinful thoughts, *"...all of us have sinned and come short of the glory of God"* (Rom. 3:23). Yet God stoops to save us. There's a word for what God does. It's called grace and it's amazing. All we need to tap into that amazing grace is faith in God – a faith like Rahab had. Trust Him and obey Him and amazing things happen.

Just look what God did with Rahab: He *"...took her tarnished portrait, cleansed it and hung it next to Sarah in the gallery of the heroes of faith (Heb. 11:1, 30, 31)."*[1] God let a saved, heathen harlot become the great grandmother of King David and an ancestor of the Messiah (Matt. 1:5).

Rahab's faith was demonstrated by a scarlet cord, and that scarlet cord is a type for Christ whose scarlet blood can save the most vile among us.

FOR DISCUSSION: The Bible record tells us Rahab was living on the city wall (Josh. 2:15), but the wall of the city collapsed according to Joshua 6:20. How does one reconcile the two verses?

[1] Pia Thompson, "Christ as the Scarlet Cord of Rahab," *the-scarlet-thread.com*

FINDING SOLACE IN CHRIST

LESSON 12

CITIES OF REFUGE

Imagine for a moment what it must have been like for so many of our immigrant ancestors to stand with pounding hearts on Ellis Island seeing for the first time the magnificent Manhattan skyline. To many who immigrated to the new world, New York City was a city of hope as were the countless cities stretching westward across America. They represented a better life and a new start. For those who awaited processing, the city of lights just across the harbor stood as a sanctuary, a haven, a city of refuge.

Nearby on Liberty Island was the Statue of Liberty which represented freedom. The statue – a gift of friendship from the people of France to the United States – had a plaque inscribed with the now famous words of Emma Lazarus:

Give me your tired, your poor,
Your huddled masses yearning to breathe free,
The wretched refuse of your teeming shore.
Send these, the homeless, tempest-tossed, to me:
I lift my lamp beside the golden door.

In many ways the cities of refuge described in the Old Testament also constituted a fresh start and a new beginning. The six cities were part of the distribution of the land among the tribes of Israel. The Levites were not given land, but instead, were given forty-eight cities spread throughout the land. Of these, six were designated as cities of refuge. The cities of refuge were towns in which those guilty of man-slaughter could seek asylum from those who sought vengeance on them. For those who fled for refuge in those six cities there was hope for the future.

The six cities were Kedesh, Shechem, Hebron, Golan, Ramoth, and Bezer. Are these cities "types" and if so what message of hope for the future did they foreshadow?

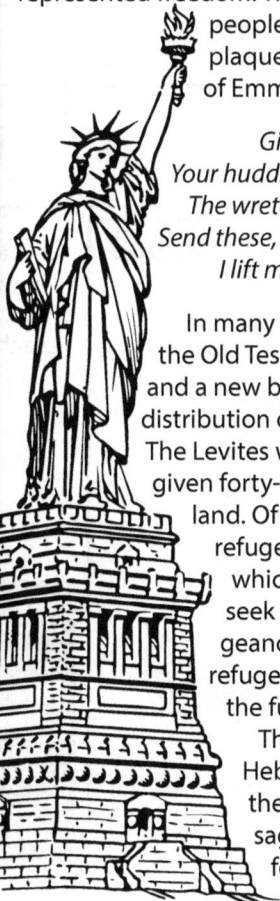

Types and Shadows - 49

For Study and Discussion

1. According to Hebrews 6:17-18 what have true believers done to take hold of the hope of salvation?

2. What was the PURPOSE of the six cities of refuge?

3. Do some research and find the meaning of the name of each city of refuge:

Kedesh

Golan

Shechem

Ramoth

Hebron

Bezer

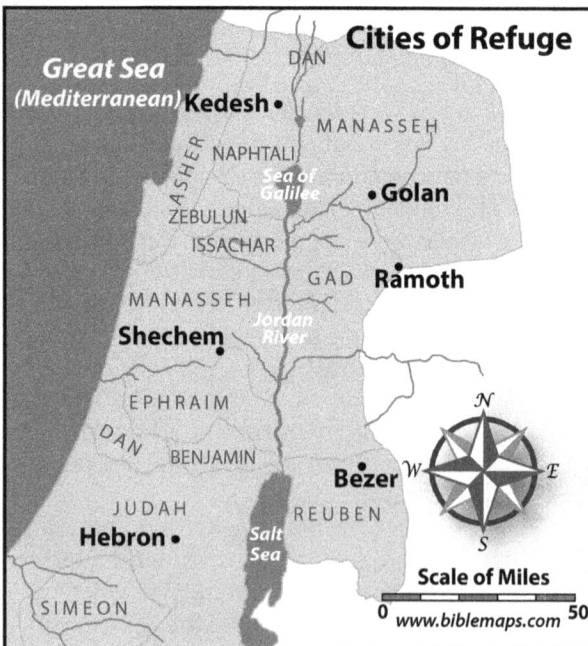

Cities of Refuge

Great Sea
(Mediterranean) **Kedesh •**
DAN
MANASSEH
ASHER
NAPHTALI
Sea of Galilee **• Golan**
ZEBULUN
ISSACHAR
GAD **Ramoth**
MANASSEH
Shechem • Jordan River
EPHRAIM
DAN
BENJAMIN
Bezer •
JUDAH
REUBEN
Hebron • Salt Sea
SIMEON
Scale of Miles
0   www.biblemaps.com   50

4. What is notable about the PLACEMENT of each city?

In commenting on the cities of refuge, Adam Clarke said the whole gospel could be preached from the particulars given of the cities of refuge. Do you agree?

5. What was the saving PROCESS to be used by a "fugitive" to gain access to a city of refuge?

6. What if anything (or anyone) do the cities of refuge foreshadow? Consider the following verses in drawing your conclusions:

• Psalms 2:11-12; 7:1; 34:22

• Jeremiah 16:18-20

• Matthew 11:28-30

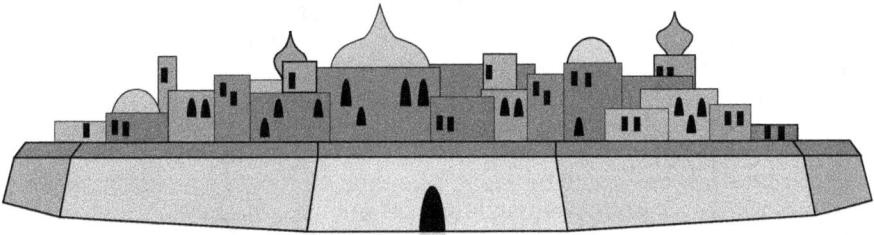

Ancient rabbis have said that to aid the fugitive it was the business of the Sanhedrin to keep the roads leading to the cities of refuge in the best possible condition. No hills were left, every river bridged, and the road itself was to be at least 48 feet wide. At every turn there were guideposts bearing the word "Refuge" and two students of the law were appointed to accompany the fleeing man and to pacify, if possible, the avenger, should he overtake the fugitive."
- *New Unger's Bible Dictionary*, 1988

Who or what is our city of refuge? (See Hebrews 12:22.)

7. Do you think Luke 3:4-6 is alluding to the cities of refuge?

Death of the High Priest

Is is it possible that within the pages of the Old Testament there are *layers* of types and shadows? In other words, could it be that types exist *within* types?* For instance, in the information about the cities of refuge we learn that the manslayer who fled to a city of refuge would have to stay in the city *until the death of the High Priest.* Imagine for a moment what it must have been like to take refuge in such a city. Yes, you are cared for and protected from the avenger, but you are likely separated from family and friends. Then – whether in a week or a decade – the High Priest dies and all transgressions are forgiven and the gates of the city are thrown open and you are free to rejoin those from whom you were separated. What a celebration that must have been!

Interestingly, then, the cities of refuge themselves seem to have been types for the solace we find in Christ, but a second layer of typology seems evident: when the High Priest died, the city's fugitive inhabitants were set free. In much the same way the death of Jesus, our High Priest, signals the liberty to be found in Him.

Nicholas Batzig in his article "Cities of Refuge" (*feedingonchrist.com*) put it this way: "The death of the High Priest was regarded, in some sense, as an atonement for the crime – for the blood that was shed. In the death of the High Priest all that the man might have done and its consequences would be wiped away and he could begin again....In all these things the Lord was planting little intimations of the way in which He brings salvation to His people."

In speaking of Christ, the Hebrew write tells us, *"...we do not have a high priest who is unable to sympathize with our weaknesses, but One who in every respect has been tempted as we are, yet without sin. Let us then with confidence draw near to the throne of grace, that we may receive mercy and find grace to help in time of need"* (Heb. 4:15-16).

It seems the Holy Spirit was so intent on our "seeing Christ" in the Old Testament that He inspired those who wrote down the Word of God to imbed types within types lest we miss the amazing message of Holy Scripture: Eternal life *only* comes through our Savior, Jesus Christ.

FOR DISCUSSION: If the cities of refuge foreshadow our own salvation and our fleeing to Christ, who then did we unintentionally kill?

---

* *Consider the following layered types: Christ is the antitype for the High Priest who entered the Holy of Holies. He is also the antitype for the animal sacrifices made by the High Priest (Exod. 30:10). Types, then, are sometimes layered within or on top of other types.*

THE GRACE OF A KING

LESSON 13

MEPHIBOSHETH

Remember the clever, English, nursery rhyme about a crooked man?

There was a crooked man and he walked a crooked mile,
He found a crooked sixpence upon a crooked stile.
He bought a crooked cat, which caught a crooked mouse.
And they all lived together in a little crooked house.

Some believe the rhyme had its origins from the history of King Charles I of England (1600–1649). The crooked man is thought to have been the Scottish General Sir Alexander Leslie who signed a covenant securing religious and political freedom for Scotland. The "crooked stile" in the poem was the jagged border between England and Scotland.

There is an obscure but beautiful story found in the pages of the Old Testament that also tells about a "crooked" person. It is a story that involves death, disability, and fear; but it is also a story about love, grace, faithfulness, and restoration because of a deep friendship and a promise.

Our final lesson in this series, then, is about a broken man with a funny name: Mephibosheth. In many ways it is also a story about each and every one of us. For, according to Paul all of us were spiritually "crooked" before we gained access to the love and grace of Christ: *"All have sinned and fallen short of the glory of God"* (Rom 3:23). The word "crook" – a vernacular term for one who is "crooked" – conveys the idea of being "bent" which itself is a term suggesting one who is not "true" or "straight" but "dishonest" or "unscrupulous."

As you reread the story of Mephibosheth in 2 Samuel 4:4; 9:1-13 pay particular attention to the sad life led by Mephibosheth that changed forever because of King David. Then, ask yourself if this story is our story revealing the amazing grace and love of our Lord and Savior, Jesus Christ.

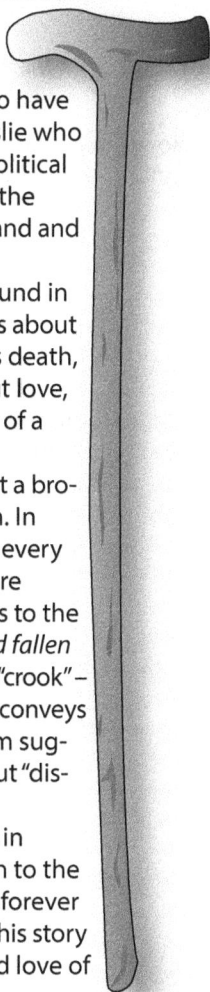

For Study and Discussion

1. According to 1 Samuel 10:8 and 13:13-14 what did Saul do that caused God to reject him as king in favor of David?

2. How would you describe the relationship between King Saul and David (1 Sam. 18:10-11; 19:9-10)?

3. How would you describe the relationship between David and Saul's son, Jonathan (1 Sam. 18:1)?

4. What promise did David and Jonathan make to each other (1 Sam. 20:1-4, 16-17, 23, 42)?

5. What happened to Saul leading to David's ascension to the throne (1 Sam. 31:1-6)?

6. Who was Jonathan's son and what happened to him (2 Sam. 4:4)?

7. Why did Mephibosheth's nurse flee? See 1 Kings 16:10-12 and 2 Kings 11:1 for a possible clue. Where did Mephibosheth end up living? What's the meaning of the town name?

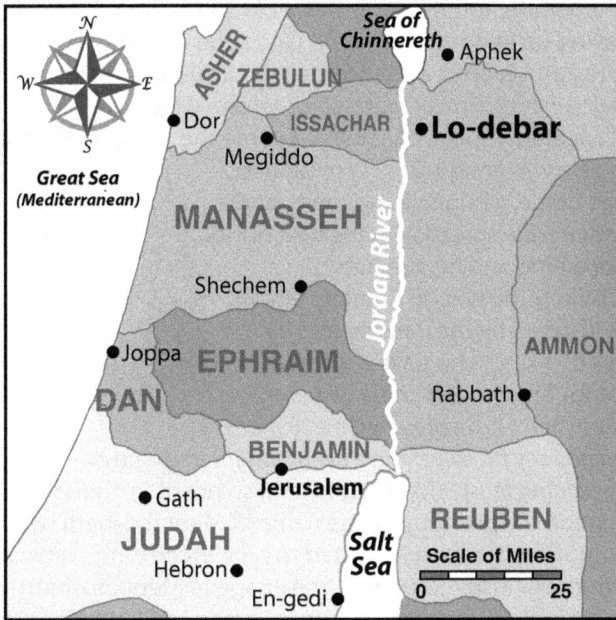

Complete the Chart Below

Consider King David's treatment of Mephibosheth in 2 Samuel 9 and indicate below any similarities you see between the grace David showed Mephibosheth and the grace enjoyed by those in Christ.

Mephibosheth	Us
Was physically bent and broken.	Rom. 3:23; 5:12 *We are bent and broken with sin.*

The King's Table

I remember fondly many of the old songs our congregation sang as I was growing up in northern Illinois. One song in particular was called "All Things Are Ready." Even at a young age I think I understood the lyricist wasn't talking about a *physical* meal, but a *spiritual* one when he repeatedly spoke of a "feast." For me the imagery was compelling: I envisioned a king's castle, a huge dining room, and a massive table spread with the best dishes fit for a King and his subjects.

It's likely the lyricist, Charles Gabriel,[1] was inspired by the parable told by Jesus of a king who gave a wedding feast for his son: *"Tell those who are invited, 'See, I have prepared my dinner, my oxen and my fat calves have been slaughtered, and everything is ready. Come to the wedding feast'"* (Matt. 22:4). It's also possible, though, that he was thinking of a poor, crippled boy by the name of Mephibosheth who was rescued from a horrible existence and invited to dine at the King's table as an adopted son.

Whatever inspired Gabriel, the image of Mephibosheth sitting at the King David's table is an amazing story of grace and love. One writer put it this way: "Mephibosheth was invited to sit at the king's table, not because of anything he had done to deserve such grace, but because of another's mercy and righteousness, so it is with the sinner."[2]

Isn't that the story of all of us who accept the Word of God and are obedient to it? Someone else has paid the price so we might be sons and daughters of the King and sit at His table and "feast upon the love of God, and drink everlasting life."

FOR DISCUSSION: We often hear it said that we are not saved by works, but is that true? Reconsider the story of Mephibosheth. Did anyone "earn" a place for Mephibosheth at the King David's table? If so who?

---

[1] Charles Gabriel sometimes used the pseudonym Charlotte Homer.
[2] "The Story of Mephibosheth," *apostolicfaithweca.org*

ANSWER KEY

What follows are some suggestions for completing the charts that appear in this workbook. I recommend you come up with your own answers before you consult these pages. Your answers may be better than mine!
- Matt Hennecke

Page 11 – Grace in the Garden Chart
He Came to us
He Called to us
He Confronted us
He Chastened us
He Covered or Clothed us

Page 14 - Noah's Ark Chart
1 builder - Christ
1 material
1 light source
1 entrance
1 household
1 refuge

Page 19 - Tower of Babel Chart
Word - the Word
A tower - Christ
Bricks/mortar - lively stones
City of men - city of God
A name - a new name
The heavens - heavenly home
Confused them - bewildered them
Scattered to stop - scattered to preach

Page 22 - Joseph Chart
Joseph was the beloved son of Jacob, Christ the beloved Son of God
Joseph's brothers rejected his rule, the Jews rejected Christ's rule
Joseph was betrayed, Christ was betrayed
Joseph was stripped of his robe, Christ was stripped of His robe
Joseph was sold for 20 pieces of silver, Christ was sold for 30 pieces of silver
Joseph was presumed dead, Christ was presumed dead
Joseph was imprisoned with two, Christ was crucified between two
Joseph 30 years old when he began (Gen. 41:46), Christ 30 years old when ministry began
Joseph sent to preserve life (Gen. 45:7), Christ sent to preserve life
Joseph called his family to come to him, Christ calls us to come to Him
Joseph essentially rose from the dead, Christ rose from the dead

Page 23 - Moses Chart
Moses born under domination of hostile power, Christ came under Roman rule
Moses born under death-of-infant decree, Christ born under death-of-infant decree
Moses had early knowledge of his mission, Christ realized His mission (Luke 2:49)
Moses voluntarily gave up glory/honor, Christ gave up equality with God
Moses was rejected by his brethren, Christ rejected by His brethren
Moses spent 40 years in seclusion away from Egypt, Christ was 40 days in wilderness
Moses commissioned to deliver God's people, Christ commissioned to seek the lost
Moses the first of the OT to work miracles, Christ the first in the NT to work miracles
Moses led God's people out of bondage, Christ leads His people out of bondage
The people were baptized into Moses (1 Cor. 10:2), People are baptized into Christ (Rom. 6:3)
Moses provided people with water (Exod. 17:6), Christ is the water of life (Rev. 21:6)

Page 27 - The Amalekites and Sin Chart
Amalekites an ever present, constant threat - Satan and sin an ever present, constant threat to us (Heb. 12:1)
Amalekites attacked the weak and infirm; where vulnerable - Satan attacks where we are vulnerable (1 Pet. 5:8)
Spoils of battle look "good" - Sin looks good to us too (Isa. 5:20)
An Amalekite claimed to kill Saul - Satan desires to kill each of us spiritually
An Amalekite took Saul's crown - Satan wants to keep us from a crown of life (James 1:12)
Haman, an Amalekite, wanted to destroy all the Jews - Satan wants to destroy all of us (Rev. 12:9)

Page 31 - The Rock and Christ Chart
The rock was solid and firm, Christ is strong and immovable
The rock was an unexpected source of water, Christ was/is an unexpected source of the water of life
The rock was in an arid wilderness, Christ gives life in a wicked, sinful world
The rock gave water abundantly to all, Christ is sufficient for all who drink of Him
The rock was appointed and given by God, Christ is appointed and given by God
The rock was smitten and life giving water came forth, Christ was smitten and spiritual life comes from Him

Page 35 - Tabernacle Chart
Entrance: Only one gate into the tabernacle (the presence of God), only one way to God the Father (John 14:6)
Brazen Altar: First step for approach to God to be cleansed by blood, so too through Christ
Laver: The priest would wash himself, we are washed in the blood of Christ through baptism
Holy Place: After a sacrifice is made and washing the priests enters the Holy Place. After Christ's sacrifice and our washing in water we enter the church.
Lampstand: The hammered gold lampstand was the source of light. Christ is the source of light (John 8:12). Interestingly the lampstand may also represent the local church which is to shine light into the world (Matt. 5:15; Rev. 1:10-12)
Table of Shewbread: Symbolic of sustenance of the 12 tribes of Israel. Christ is the bread of life for spiritual Israel
Altar of Incense: A type of prayer. A fragrant aroma ascending to God.
Veil: "Therefore, brothers, since we have confidence to enter the Most Holy Place by the blood of Jesus, by a new and living way opened for us through the curtain, that is, his body ...let us draw near to God with a sincere heart in full assurance of faith" (Heb. 10:19-22).
Holy of Holies: We can now boldly enter into God's presence, "the inner sanctuary behind the curtain, where Jesus, who went before us, has entered on our behalf" (Heb. 6:19-20).

Page 38 - The Lampstand
The Lampstand:
Material - PURE GOLD (Exod. 25:31)
The material of the lampstand should also be the spiritual material of the church.
Craftsmanship - HAMMERED WORK (Exod. 25:31,36)
The craftsmanship of the lampstand is in many ways the spiritual craftsmanship of the church. Sound local churches will be hammered by persecution. 1 Peter 1:7 says - "the trial of your faith, being much more precious than of gold."
Uniformity - ONE PIECE (Exod. 25:31)
The uniformity of the lampstand is also to be the spiritual uniformity of the church. Psalm 133:1 says - "Behold, how good and how pleasant it is for brethren to dwell together in unity."
Purpose - SHEDDING LIGHT (Exod. 25:37)
The purpose of the lampstand in the tabernacle which represented Christ, is also the spiritual purpose of local congregations. Local churches are to hold forth the light of the gospel.
Warning - MADE AFTER GOD'S PATTERN (Exod. 25:40)
The warning about the lampstand is also a warning to the local church. Local churches are to follow the pattern, the explicit instructions of God in work and worship.

Page 38 - The Paschal Lamb
For even Christ our passover is sacrificed for us. – 1 Cor. 5:7
• An Emblem of Innocence
• Without Blemish
• A Year Old Male - A one year old male lamb was in its prime. Christ had just come to the ripeness of manhood when he was offered.
• The Manner of Death - The lamb was not to have a bone of its body broken. While many sacrifices were made

Page 39 - The Ark of the Covenant
On top of the ark of the covenant was a lid called the "mercy-seat." In a manner of speaking, the mercy-seat concealed from God's view the ever-condemning judgment of the Law. Note that the tablets of the ten commandments were one of the items kept inside the ark - they represented the Law. Christ intercedes between the Law and God for us. He "covers" our transgressions of the Law, thus allowing us access to God.

Page 39 - The Scapegoat
Two young goats were selected by the casting of lots. One goat was "for the Lord." One goat was to be the scapegoat. The Hebrew word for scapegoat is *azazel* – "goat of departure" – a rare Hebrew noun meaning "dismissal" or "entire removal." When we view the Lord's goat and the scapegoat as one atonement offering, rather than two separate offerings, we can understand and appreciate the symbolic fulfillment more readily. Jesus is the perfect fulfillment of the typical atonement sacrifice. As the Lord's scapegoat, His blood cleansed the heavenly sanctuary (Heb. 9:23). As the scapegoat, He bore our sins and took them away forever.

Page 43 - Leprosy Chart
Leprosy starts small - so too does sin
Leprosy is deeper than the skin - so too sin
Untreated leprosy spreads - so too sin
Leprosy defiles the body - so too sin (individually and within the local church)
Leprosy separates us for others - sin separates us from God
Leprosy is curable - so too sin
To be rendered clean blood must be shed - for us to be rendered clean blood was shed

Page 47 - Rahab Chart
Rahab's Condition and Salvation is like ours in that...
1. Her CONDITION and OURS: She was doomed
2. Her CONDUCT and OURS: She demonstrated a desire for salvation
3. Her CONFESSION and OURS: She declared God to be LORD (convenant term Jehovah)
4. Her CONSECRATION and OURS: She was "set apart" for salvation by the scarlet cord. Interesting that the sign was red and on the window. Looking back, this was reminiscent of the Passover wherein blood was put on the doorway to mark or set apart those who would be spared destruction by the angel of death. Looking forward the scarlet cord is reminiscent of the crimson-stained cross marking the entry into the Lord's church provided by Christ's blood and our contact with its saving power through obedience (Rom. 6).
5. Her COMPANY and OURS. The crimson cord was not enough. Rahab and her family had to go INTO the house, and remain IN the house. She and her family became part of the house of faith, Israel. Similarly we must be IN Christ and remain IN Christ (Gal.3:27).

Page 55 - Mephibosheth Chart
Mephibosheth was physically bent and broken - We are spiritually bent and broken by sin
Mephibosheth lived in a sad, forsaken place - We live in an evil and godless world
Mephibosheth was the blessed recipient of a promise - We are the recipients of a better promise
Mephibosheth "earned" a place at the King's table by Jonathan - We earn a place at God's table by Christ
Mephibosheth was treated as a son of the King - We are adopted sons of God by faith
Mephibosheth gave the King honor and allegiance - We must honor our King

NOTES